identity

DISCOVERING WHO YOU ARE

Published by Skinny Brown Dog Media
Atlanta, GA /Punta del Este, Uruguay

For Information, Contact:
Distributed by Skinny Brown Dog Media
SkinnyBrownDogMedia.com
Email: Info@SkinnyBrownDogMedia.com

Identity
Discovering Who You Are
By Eric G Reid
Part of the Whole Life Devotional Series

Library of Congress Cataloging in Publication Data
ISBN (eBook):   978-1-965235-18-8
ISBN (trade paperback):   978-1-965235-15-7
ISBN (Hardback Dust Jacketed):   978-1-965235-16-4
ISBN (case laminate):   978-1-965235-17-1

CONTENTS

WEEK 1
Discovering Your Identity in Christ

WEEK 2
LIVING OUT YOUR GODLY IDENTITY

WEEK 3
EMBRACING YOUR ROLE
AS A LEADER AND LIGHT

DEDICATION

To the Men of the 12 Stone Church Wednesday AM Small Group,
Your unwavering support, bold questions, and weekly
fellowship continually shape and inspire me.
Your courage to ask,
"Whose am I?" leads us all closer to truth and purpose.
Thank you for walking this journey with me.

"As iron sharpens iron, so one person sharpens another."
—Proverbs 27:17

Identity

Welcome to "Identity: Discovering Who You Are," a three-week devotional designed to help you discover and embrace your true identity. Through daily scripture readings, reflections, questions, and actionable steps, this study aims to guide you on a journey of spiritual growth and self-discovery.

In a world constantly vying for our attention and approval, it's easy to lose sight of who we truly are. We often find ourselves conforming to societal standards, seeking validation from others, and defining our worth by external achievements. This devotional is an invitation to step away from those pressures and look inward, to understand our true selves as seen through the eyes of our Creator.

Over the next three weeks, we will delve into the foundational truths about our identity in Christ. Each day's devotional is crafted to help you reflect on key scriptures that reveal God's perspective on who you are. You will be encouraged to meditate on these truths, allowing them to sink deeply into your heart and mind. The reflections and questions are designed to challenge you, provoke thought, and prompt meaningful conversations with God and others.

This devotional is not just about gaining knowledge; it's about transformation. Each day includes practical steps you can take to apply what you've learned, helping you to live out your true identity in your everyday life. Whether it's through prayer, journaling, or specific actions, these steps are meant to reinforce the truths you are discovering and to help you build habits that support your spiritual growth.

You will also find that this journey is not meant to be taken alone. Sharing your insights and experiences with a trusted friend or small group can enhance your understanding and provide mutual encouragement. As you walk through these three weeks, consider inviting someone to join you, creating a space for accountability and deeper connection.

Remember, discovering your true identity is a lifelong journey. This devotional is a step along the path, equipping you with tools and insights to continue growing in your understanding of who you are in Christ. Embrace this time with an open heart, willing to be transformed by the truths you will encounter.

May this journey lead you to a deeper awareness of your worth and purpose, firmly rooted in the unchanging love and truth of God. Let's embark on this transformative journey together, discovering the fullness of our identity as beloved children of God.

Why This Study?

In today's fast paced and everchanging world, many of us struggle with questions of identity. We are constantly bombarded with messages from the media, society, and even our own social circles about who we should be and what we should aspire to. These worldly influences can often lead us away from our true identity, creating confusion, dissatisfaction, and a sense of emptiness.

Our identities can be shaped by external pressures that push us towards conformity and away from authenticity. The constant comparison to others, driven by social media and cultural expectations, can create an illusion that we are never enough. This relentless pursuit of approval and validation from others can leave us feeling hollow and disconnected from our true selves.

Moreover, the rapid pace of technological advancements and societal changes can exacerbate feelings of instability and insecurity. In a world where trends and norms shift swiftly, it's easy to lose sight of the core of who we are. This study aims to anchor you in the unchanging truth of your identity in Christ, providing a solid foundation amidst the turbulence of modern life.

The Importance of Identity

Your identity shapes how you see yourself, how you interact with others, and how you navigate the world. When your identity is rooted in God, it provides a solid foundation that stands firm amidst the shifting sands of life. Discovering who you are in Christ brings clarity, purpose, and a deep sense of belonging. It allows you to live confidently, knowing that you are loved and valued by the Creator of the universe.

In contrast, when your identity is influenced by worldly standards and expectations, it can lead to instability and a lack of fulfillment. Worldly identity is often based on external factors such as appearance, achievements, and social status. These factors are transient and can change rapidly, leaving you feeling uncertain and insecure. By grounding your identity in God, you can experience a sense of peace and stability that transcends the ups and downs of life.

What Can Be Gained?

Engaging with this study offers numerous benefits:

1. Clarity and Confidence: By understanding your identity in Christ, you will gain clarity about your purpose and direction in life. This newfound clarity will empower you to make decisions confidently and live with a sense of intentionality and purpose.
2. Spiritual Growth: Daily engagement with scripture and reflective questions will deepen your relationship with God. As you spend time in prayer and meditation, you will become more attuned to His voice and guidance.
3. Resilience Against Worldly Pressures: By recognizing and resisting the influences of worldly identity, you will develop resilience. This will help you stand firm in your faith, even when faced with challenges
    and temptations.
4. Authentic Community: Understanding the importance of community and support in your spiritual journey will encourage you to build and maintain meaningful relationships with fellow believers. These connections will provide encouragement, accountability, and a sense of belonging.
5. Practical Application: Each day's action plan provides practical steps to apply what you've learned, making the principles of a godly identity a tangible part of your daily life. This will help you integrate your faith into every aspect of your existence.
6. Inner Peace and Joy: Discovering and living out your true identity in God brings a profound sense of peace and joy. You will experience the contentment that comes from knowing you are loved and valued by your Creator, and that your life has a meaningful purpose.

Journey of Transformation

This study is not just about gaining knowledge; it is about transformation. As you work through each day's readings and reflections, allow the Holy Spirit to work in your heart and mind. Be open to the changes that God wants to make in your life. Embrace the process of becoming who He has created you to be.

Transformation requires intentionality. It involves making a conscious effort to align your thoughts, attitudes, and actions with God's truth. This study will guide you through this process, providing the tools and support you need to grow and mature in your faith.

How to Use This Devotional

Each day of this devotional is structured to provide a holistic approach to understanding and embracing your identity in God. Here's how to make the most of it:

1. Scripture Readings: Begin each day by reading the suggested scriptures. Take your time to read and reflect on the passages, allowing God's Word to speak to your heart.
2. Devotional Thought: Read the devotional thought for the day. These reflections are designed to help you understand and apply the scriptures to your life. Spend time journaling about what you've read and how it resonates with you. Use the journal prompts to guide your reflections and capture your thoughts and feelings.
3. Questions for Reflection: Spend time pondering the reflection questions. These questions are meant to provoke deep thought and personal application. Consider journaling your responses to capture your insights and growth.

4. Daily Action Plan: Each day includes a practical action step to help you live out the principles you've learned. These actions will reinforce your understanding and encourage you to integrate godly identity into your daily life.

5. Prayer: End each day with a time of prayer. Ask God to help you embrace your identity in Him and to guide you in living out His purpose for your life.

Purpose vs. Identity

It is crucial to understand the difference between purpose and identity as you delve into this study. Identity is who you are at your core, defined by your relationship with God and your inherent qualities as His creation. Your identity is constant and unchanging, rooted in being a child of God, loved and valued by Him.

Purpose, on the other hand, is about what you do with your life. It is the specific calling or mission that God has for you, shaped by your talents, passions, and the unique opportunities He places in your path. While your purpose may evolve and change over time, it is always influenced by your identity in Christ.

Your identity in God profoundly influences your purpose. When you understand who you are in Him, you gain clarity about what you are meant to do. A strong sense of identity provides the foundation for discovering and pursuing your purpose with confidence and conviction. By aligning your actions with your godly identity, you ensure that your purpose is not swayed by worldly pressures but remains true to God's plan for your life.

It's important to uncover or rediscover our true identity and disconnect from roles and labels such as "husband," "father," "son," "doctor," "plumber," or even a "Minnesota Gophers fan." These roles,

while significant, are not the essence of who we are. Instead, our true
identity lies in being a beloved child of God

Encouragement for the Journey

As you embark on this journey, remember that finding
and embracing your godly identity is a process. It requires patience,
reflection, and a willingness to be transformed by God's Word. In this
world that often seems to put us at war with ourselves and our beliefs,
the journey is the only way
to victory.

There is a Chinese proverb that states, 知己知彼，百战不殆
(Zhī jǐ zhī bǐ, bǎi zhàn bù dài) "Know yourself, know your enemy, and
you will never be defeated in a hundred battles." Understanding who
you are, and recognizing the forces that challenge your faith are crucial
steps in this journey. By knowing your true identity and the spiritual
battles you face, you can stand firm and secure in God's promises.

Let this study be a guide to help you draw closer to God,
understand yourself better, and live out the unique identity He has
given you. Embrace this opportunity to grow in your faith and discover
the depths of God's love for you. Allow His truth to shape your identity
and guide your steps. Trust that as you seek Him, He will reveal His
purpose for your life and empower you to live it out fully.

Welcome to a journey of transformation and discovery. May
God bless you richly as you seek to understand and embrace your true
identity in Him.

WEEK 1
Discovering Your Identity in Christ

Hey there, friends. Ever caught yourself staring in the mirror, wondering, "Who am I, really?" I've been there more times than I can count.

There was a time when I defined myself by my job, my achievements, and what others thought of me. Those childhood nicknames (like "dumber than whale poop Eric") shaped my choices well into adulthood. Before I knew it, I was trapped in unfulfilling jobs and relationships, feeling lost and disconnected from my true self.

It wasn't until a counselor challenged me with a simple question: "Who are you, outside of all those titles and roles?" That's when my journey to discover my true identity began. And let me tell you, it wasn't always easy, but it has been worth it.

I started to realize that my identity wasn't dependent on others' definitions or expectations. It was rooted in something much deeper – in who I was created to be.

Welcome to the first week of our journey into discovering our true identity. This week, we're laying the foundation for understanding who we are in God's eyes. Together, we'll explore biblical truths about our creation, our status as children of God, and what it means to be made in His image.

In a world that constantly tells us who we should be, it's vital to ground ourselves in the truth of who God says we are. We'll focus on understanding the profound love and purpose God has for each of us. Remember, we're not defined by our past, our achievements, or others' opinions. We're defined by God's unwavering love and His intention in creating us.

As we dive into Scripture, we'll see that being children of God means we're loved unconditionally, accepted fully, and valued immensely. To be made in God's image is to reflect His character and attributes, giving us a sense of purpose and direction.

By the end of this week, my hope is that we'll have a deeper understanding of what it means to be a new creation in Christ. We're talking about embracing the new life He offers, letting go of old identities that no longer serve us.

So, are you ready to start this identity adventure? It might be challenging at times, but I promise it'll be eye opening and ultimately transformative. Let's take this journey together!

Key Themes

- Being a Child of God
- Made in God's Image
- Becoming a New Creation

Anchor Scripture

"Therefore if anyone is in Christ, the new creation has come: The old has gone, the new is here!"
—2 Corinthians 5:17

Reflection

As we embark on this week, let's consider together what it means to be created in God's image and to be called His children. Reflect on how these truths impact our daily lives and self-perception. Let's take time to meditate on God's unconditional love and how it redefines our identity.

DAY 1
WHAT IS IDENTITY?

Have you ever looked in the mirror and wondered, "Who am I really?"

Do you remember those awkward teenage years when you were trying to figure out who you were? For me, it involved a lot of bad fashion choices and a quest to fit in with the cool crowd. As I grew older, it became more about my job title and the income I earned. Now, as an adult, the question of identity has taken on a deeper, more spiritual meaning. It's not just about fitting in but about understanding who we are in the eyes of God.

Welcome to the first week of our journey together into discovering our true identity in Christ. We'll explore the biblical truths about our creation, our status as children of God, and what it means to be made in His image. Our goal is to replace the world's misconceptions with the solid truth of God's Word.

In a world that constantly tells us who we should be, it's vital for us to ground ourselves in the truth of who God says we are. By the end of this week, we will have a deeper understanding of what it means to be a new creation in Christ, shedding the old and embracing the new life He offers.

Get ready to uncover the beautiful truth of your God-given identity. It's a journey worth taking, and I'm thrilled to be on it with you.

Role Models in Scripture

Consider the life of David, the shepherd boy who became king. Despite his humble beginnings, David understood his identity as a child of God. This understanding gave him the confidence to face Goliath, lead a nation, and write many of the Psalms.

David's courage in facing Goliath wasn't based on his own strength but on his unwavering faith in God's power and his identity as God's chosen one. When the entire Israelite army trembled in fear, David, fueled by his unshakeable faith in God, stepped forward. Despite his youth and lack of military experience, he declared, "*The Lord who rescued me from the paw of the lion and the paw of the bear will rescue me from the hand of this Philistine*" (1 Samuel 17:37). Armed with just a sling and five smooth stones, David confronted Goliath. He didn't rely on his own strength or abilities but on the power of God. With a single stone, he struck down the giant, securing victory for Israel.

David's faith didn't just make him brave; it made him victorious. His story shows us that faith in God can turn the most unlikely individuals into mighty warriors for His kingdom. David's identity in God gave him the courage to face his fears and the enemies of his people. His reliance on God's strength over his own teaches us a powerful lesson about finding our identity in God.

David's life continued to reflect his deep faith even after becoming king. As king, he faced numerous challenges, from personal failures to political threats. Yet, his psalms reveal a man who continually sought God's presence, guidance, and forgiveness. David's story encourages us to find our identity in God, which empowers us to face our giants, lead with integrity, and worship God with our whole hearts. Despite his faults and failures, David always returned to God, seeking His mercy and grace. This continual return to God's presence and his reliance on God's identity over his own is what made David a man after God's own heart.

David's life illustrates the journey of identity discovery and affirmation. He shows us that knowing oneself in God, understanding one's divine identity, is crucial to overcoming life's battles. As Ephesians 6:1011 says, *"Finally, be strong in the Lord and in his mighty power. Put on the full armor of God, so that you can take your stand against the devil's schemes."* David knew his identity in God and understood the enemy he faced. This knowledge and faith made him victorious.

Let David's story be a guide as you seek to understand your true identity in God. Remember, your identity is not in your accomplishments, roles, or titles, but in being a beloved child of God. Embrace this identity, and you too can face your giants with confidence and emerge victorious.

Scripture to Remember

"Then God said, 'Let us make mankind in our image, in our likeness...'"
—Genesis 1:2627

"What is mankind that you are mindful of them, human beings that you care for them?"
—Psalm 8:45

"For we are God's handiwork, created in Christ Jesus to do good works..."
—Ephesians 2:10

Consider This

Reflect on being created in God's image and the significance of this for our identity. Think about how David's understanding of his identity in God gave him the courage to face challenges and lead with integrity. Spend time journaling about how being made in God's image shapes your view of yourself and your capabilities.

Questions for Reflection

1. What does it mean to you that you are made in God's image?

_____

_____

_____

2. How does this shape your view of yourself?

_____

_____

_____

3. In what areas of your life do you struggle to see God's image in yourself, and how can you change that perspective?

_____

_____

_____

Living Into Our Identity

Write down three ways you see God's image in yourself and thank Him for these gifts.

_____

_____

_____

_____

_____

Building Deeper Connection to Faith

- Journaling Prompt: Reflect on the qualities that show you are made in God's image.
- Prayer: "Heavenly Father, thank You for creating me in Your image. Help me to see myself through Your eyes and to live out my purpose with confidence and faith. Amen."

Tomorrow's Journey

Today, we've laid the first stone in the foundation of our identity by understanding our creation in God's image. Tomorrow, we will delve into the relationship between our identity and Christ, and how this transforms our lives.

DAY 2
IDENTITY IN CHRIST

When I first became a Christian, I was filled with excitement but also overwhelmed by the changes I thought I needed to make. I believed I had to transform everything about myself overnight, and when I inevitably failed, I felt disheartened. At church, I wore my "Christian mask," trying to appear perfect, but at home, I felt like a fraud. The desire to be a good Christian was strong, yet I constantly fell short and berated myself for every mistake.

However, I soon discovered that my identity in Christ wasn't about an external transformation but an inside out change. God loved me unconditionally, even amidst my mess and failures. This realization marked the beginning of genuine transformation. Although the process was far from perfect and I continued to stumble, I learned to extend grace to myself and persist in my journey.

Reflecting on my past, I can see significant growth, despite the challenges. Becoming who God created me to be is a lifelong journey that demands patience, perseverance, and an abundance of grace. It's about embracing God's love and allowing it to reshape me from within.

Role Models in Scripture

The Apostle Paul, formerly Saul, had a radical transformation upon encountering Christ. His new identity in Christ changed his life's mission from persecuting Christians to spreading the gospel. Paul's letters in the New Testament are powerful reminders of the transformative power of understanding our identity in Christ.

Once a fervent persecutor of Christians, Paul's encounter with Jesus on the road to Damascus redefined his identity. From that moment, Paul saw himself not as a defender of the old law but as an ambassador of Christ. This new identity fueled his missionary journeys, his letters to the churches, and his unwavering commitment to spreading the gospel despite immense persecution.

In his letter to the Galatians, Paul shares, *"I have been crucified with Christ and I no longer live, but Christ lives in me. The life I now live in the body, I live by faith in the Son of God, who loved me and gave himself for me"* (Galatians 2:20). This statement encapsulates the essence of our identity in Christ – it's no longer about us, but about Christ living in and through us. Paul's story teaches us that no matter our past, our identity in Christ can redefine our future and purpose. It reminds us that being in Christ means being a new creation, leaving behind the old and embracing the new life and mission God has for us.

Paul's transformation is a testament to the power of God's grace. Despite his past, God chose Paul to be a key figure in the spread of Christianity. This shows us that our past does not disqualify us from being used by God. Instead, our identity in Christ makes us valuable and capable of fulfilling God's purposes.

Scripture to Remember

"Therefore, if anyone is in Christ, the new creation has come: The old has gone, the new is here!"
—2 Corinthians 5:17

"I have been crucified with Christ and I no longer live, but Christ lives in me."
—Galatians 2:20

"For you died, and your life is now hidden with Christ in God."
—Colossians 3:3

Consider This

Understanding our new identity in Christ as a new creation. Reflect on Paul's transformation and how his new identity in Christ changed his life's mission. Spend time journaling about the changes you have experienced since knowing Christ. Consider what aspects of your old identity you have left behind and how your life has changed.

Questions for Reflection

1. How has your life changed since knowing Christ?

_____

_____

_____

2. What aspects of your old identity have you left behind?

_____

_____

_____

3. What parts of you are you unresolved with?

_____

_____

_____

Living Into Our Identity

Identify and pray about one area where you struggle to embrace your new identity in Christ.

_____

_____

_____

_____

_____

Building Deeper Connection to Faith

- **Journaling Prompt**: Write about a time when you experienced God's grace in a moment of failure. How did it change your perspective and actions?
- **Prayer**: "Heavenly Father, thank You for Your unconditional love and grace. Help me to embrace my identity in You and to extend that grace to myself and others. Guide me in my

journey of transformation, and let Your love shape me from the inside out. Amen."

Tomorrow's Journey

Today, we've explored the transformative power of our identity in Christ. Tomorrow, we'll examine how worldly influences can affect our sense of identity and how to resist them.

DAY 3
WORLDLY IDENTITY

When I was younger, I was always trying to fit in with the popular crowd. The problem was the popular crowd was always changing. I became consumed with dressing like them, talking like them, and trying to like what they liked. But no matter how hard I tried, I never truly felt like I belonged. The outside looked right, but the inside was in turmoil. I constantly felt unworthy of pretty much everything good that came into my life. I became so consumed with protecting my image that I lost myself. It wasn't until I started to understand my identity in Christ that I began to feel a sense of belonging and purpose.

The more I chased after the approval of others, the more disconnected I felt from my true self. I was living a life dictated by external validations, and each day felt like a performance where I played a role that wasn't truly mine. The constant pressure to conform to everchanging standards left me exhausted and empty. The worst part was that I was hiding my true struggles, afraid that my flaws would make me even more unworthy in the eyes of those I desperately wanted to impress.

As I explored deeper who I was in Christ, a slow awareness began to dawn on me. My worth wasn't determined by the approval of others but by the love of God. This realization didn't come overnight;

it was a gradual process of letting go of my fears and embracing the truth that I am fearfully and wonderfully made (Psalm 139:14). This truth started to reshape my identity from the inside out. I no longer needed to strive for perfection or hide my imperfections. God's unconditional love and acceptance gave me the freedom to be authentic and vulnerable.

Understanding my identity in Christ brought a growing sense of belonging. I learned that my value doesn't fluctuate with the opinions of others but is firmly rooted in being a beloved child of God. This shift in perspective not only relieved the pressure to conform but also allowed me to discover my true passions and purpose. I began to live not for the fleeting applause of the world but for the eternal approval of my Creator.

Role Models in Scripture

Consider King Solomon, who had immense wisdom, wealth, and power. Despite all his achievements, he recognized the emptiness of worldly pursuits. In Ecclesiastes, Solomon reflects on the vanity of worldly success and the importance of fearing God and keeping His commandments.

Solomon's life began with great promise; God granted him unparalleled wisdom. His reign was marked by peace and prosperity, and he built the magnificent temple in Jerusalem. However, Solomon's later years were marred by his pursuit of worldly pleasures, which led him away from God. He writes in Ecclesiastes, *I have seen all the things that are done under the sun; all of them are meaningless, a chasing after the wind"* (Ecclesiastes 1:14). Despite his vast wealth and accomplishments, Solomon realized that without a relationship with God, everything was meaningless.

In his later years, Solomon's reflections are a sobering reminder of the emptiness of worldly success. He concludes, *"Now all has been heard; here is the conclusion of the matter: Fear God and keep his commandments, for this is the duty of all mankind"* (Ecclesiastes 12:13). Solomon's honest reflections remind us that our true fulfillment comes from our identity in God, not from the fleeting pursuits of this world. His life teaches us the importance of prioritizing our relationship with God over worldly achievements.

Scripture to Remember

"For you created my inmost being; you knit me together in my mother's womb. I praise you because I am fearfully and wonderfully made; your works are wonderful, I know that full well."
—Psalm 139:1314

"So God created mankind in his own image, in the image of God he created them; male and female he created them."
—Genesis 1:27

"Yet to all who did receive him, to those who believed in his name, he gave the right to become children of God."
—John 1:12

Consider This

Reflect on your own journey of seeking approval and how it has impacted your sense of identity. How has understanding your worth in Christ brought you peace and a sense of belonging? Think about the areas in your life where you still feel the pressure to conform and how you can lean into your identity in Christ to find freedom.

Questions for Reflection

1. In what ways have you tried to conform to others' expectations, and how has this affected your sense of identity?

_____

_____

_____

2. How has understanding your identity in Christ changed the way you view yourself and your worth?

_____

_____

_____

3. What steps can you take to live more authentically in your identity as a child of God, free from the need for external validation?

_____

_____

_____

Living Into Our Identity

Identify one area in your life where you feel the most pressure to conform and make a conscious effort to embrace your true identity in Christ in that area.

_____

_____

_____

_____

_____

Building Deeper Connection to Faith

- **Journaling Prompt**: Write about a time when you felt pressured to conform and how understanding your identity in Christ helped you overcome that pressure.
- **Prayer**: "Heavenly Father, thank You for creating me in Your image and for loving me unconditionally. Help me to see myself through Your eyes and to live out my true identity with confidence and grace. Free me from the need for external validation and anchor my worth in Your eternal love. Amen."

Tomorrow's Journey

Today, we've explored the impact of seeking approval on our sense of identity and the peace that comes from understanding our worth in Christ. Tomorrow, we will delve deeper into how our identity in Christ shapes our purpose and actions in the world.

DAY 4
DISCOVERING YOUR GOD GIVEN IDENTITY

Have you ever felt like you just don't fit in? Like you're trying to be someone you're not? I've been there. There was a time when I felt so lost, I couldn't have found my way with a map and a compass. I was living someone else's life, trying to be the person I thought everyone wanted me to be. It was exhausting, and it left me feeling empty.

But here's the thing: this struggle is more common than we might think. Many of us go through periods where we're unsure of who we really are. The good news is that the Bible is full of examples that can help us navigate these feelings and find our true path. It's like having a spiritual guide leading us back to our God-given purpose.

If you're feeling lost right now, don't lose heart. Even those of us who sometimes feel directionless can find our way with God's guidance. It might take time, and there might be a few detours along the way, but that's all part of the journey.

Remember, God has a mission for you. He created you with intention and discovering that purpose is one of life's greatest adventures. It's like peeling back layers to reveal the incredible person He designed you to be.

Role Models in Scripture

Moses' life reads like an ancient soap opera with a divine twist. Picture this: A Hebrew baby, raised as an Egyptian prince, living the high life in Pharaoh's palace. Talk about an identity crisis waiting to happen!

Now, I don't know about you, but if I'd grown up with golden sandals and servants at my beck and call, I might've been tempted to stick with that gig. But Moses? He chose a different path. He embraced his true identity as a Hebrew and, more importantly, as a servant of God. That's some serious character right there!

His journey from palace playboy to wilderness wanderer to freedom fighting leader is like the ultimate makeover show, but instead of a new wardrobe, Moses got a whole new purpose.

Remember that burning bush moment? That was God's way of saying, "Hey Moses, I've got big plans for you!" And Moses, bless his heart, basically replied, "Uh, God, I think you've got the wrong number." Classic case of imposter syndrome, am I right? But God wasn't having any of it. He knew exactly who Moses was meant to be.

Despite feeling about as qualified as a fish teaching bicycle riding, Moses stepped up to the plate. He confronted Pharaoh (his former family, mind you talk about awkward family reunions!), led the Israelites out of slavery, and even parted a sea. All because he finally understood and embraced who God created him to be.

Now, I'm not saying we're all destined to part seas or lead nations (though if that's your calling, go for it!). But Moses' story teaches us something crucial: our true identity and purpose aren't found in our job titles, our bank accounts, or even our family backgrounds. They're found in God.

Think about it how often do we define ourselves by what we do rather than who we are in God's eyes? I know I've been guilty of this.

But Moses' life shows us that when we embrace our God-given identity, we're capable of far more than we ever imagined.

So, the next time you're feeling lost or unsure of your purpose, remember Moses. Remember that God sees the real you the you He created with a specific purpose in mind. And trust me, His plans for you are far greater than anything you could dream up on your own.

Are you ready to embrace your true identity and step into the purpose God has for you? It might not involve a burning bush or a staff that turns into a snake (thankfully), but I guarantee it'll be an adventure worth taking. Let's follow Moses' lead and start living out our God-given identities. Who knows? You might just find yourself doing things you never thought possible!

Scriptures to Remember

"For you created my inmost being; you knit me together in my mother's womb. I praise you because I am fearfully and wonderfully made; your works are wonderful, I know that full well."
—Psalm 139:1314

"So God created mankind in his own image, in the image of God he created them; male and female he created them."
—Genesis 1:27

"Yet to all who did receive him, to those who believed in his name, he gave the right to become children of God."
—John 1:12

Consider This

Reflect on your own journey of seeking approval and how it has impacted your sense of identity. How has understanding your worth in Christ brought you peace and a sense of belonging? Think about the areas in your life where you still feel the pressure to conform and how you can lean into your identity in Christ to find freedom.

Questions for Reflection

1. In what ways have you tried to conform to others' expectations, and how has this affected your sense of identity?

_____

_____

_____

2. How has understanding your identity in Christ changed the way you view yourself and your worth?

_____

_____

_____

3. What steps can you take to live more authentically in your identity as a child of God, free from the need for external validation?

_____

_____

_____

Living Into Our Identity

Identify one area in your life where you feel the most pressure to conform and make a conscious effort to embrace your true identity in Christ in that area.

_____

_____

_____

_____

_____

Building Deeper Connection to Faith

- **Journaling Prompt**: Write about a time when you felt pressured to conform and how understanding your identity in Christ helped you overcome that pressure.
- **Prayer**: "Heavenly Father, thank You for creating me in Your image and for loving me unconditionally. Help me to see myself through Your eyes and to live out my true identity with confidence and grace. Free me from the need for external validation and anchor my worth in Your eternal love. Amen."

DAY 5
IDENTITY AFFIRMATION

cue existential crisis Have you ever found yourself staring at the ceiling at 2 AM, pondering the meaning of life and questioning your very existence? Just me? Okay, cool. But seriously, have you ever wondered why you're here and what your life is meant to accomplish? Because same.

Well, buckle up, buttercup, because I've got some good news for you. Affirming our identity in God is like finding the secret cheat code to life, except instead of unlimited lives, we get the power to make a real difference in the world. It's the key to unlocking our ultimate destiny and fulfilling our divine purpose.

So, if you're ready to trade in your existential dread for some divine inspiration, let's explore how embracing who we are in God can give us the courage to step up and make our mark on the world. Get ready to swap your "why me?" for a "why not me?" and let's do this! It's time to stop questioning your existence and start living the life you were meant to live.

Role Models in Scripture

Esther, a Jewish orphan who became queen of Persia, had to affirm her identity when facing the challenge of saving her people. Her courage and faith in God's plan for her life are testaments to the power of embracing and affirming our identity in God.

Esther's rise to queenship seemed like a fairy tale, but it was her moment of crisis that truly defined her. When Haman plotted to destroy the Jews, Esther had to choose between hiding her identity and risking her life to save her people. Mordecai challenged Esther with these words: *"And who knows but that you have come to your royal position for such a time as this?"* (Esther 4:14). Esther's response, *"If I perish, I perish"* (Esther 4:16), shows the strength and resolve that came from embracing her identity and God-given purpose.

Despite the potential consequences, Esther chose to trust God. Her bravery reminds us that affirming our identity in God can lead to actions that change lives and fulfill divine purposes. Esther's example encourages us to stand firm in our identity, even when it's difficult, and trust that God has placed us where we are for a reason. Her bravery and faith are powerful reminders that God's plans for us are greater than our fears.

Scriptures to Remember

"For you created my inmost being; you knit me together in my mother's womb. I praise you because I am fearfully and wonderfully made; your works are wonderful, I know that full well."
—Psalm 139:1314

"Before I formed you in the womb I knew you, before you were born I set you apart; I appointed you as a prophet to the nations."
—Jeremiah 1:5

"For he chose us in him before the creation of the world to
be holy and blameless in his sight. In love he predestined
us for adoption to sonship through Jesus Christ, in
accordance with his pleasure and will."
—Ephesians 1:45

Consider This

Recognize that you are fearfully and wonderfully made. Reflect on Esther's courage in affirming her identity and fulfilling her purpose. Spend time journaling about how knowing you are wonderfully made by God impacts your self-esteem and daily living. Write a letter to yourself affirming your God-given identity and keep it for future encouragement.

Questions for Reflection

1. How does knowing you are wonderfully made by God impact your self-esteem and daily living?

_____

_____

_____

2. In what ways can Esther's story inspire you to embrace and affirm your identity in God?

_____

_____

_____

3. How can you trust God's plan for your life, even when it's difficult to see the path ahead?

_____

_____

_____

Living Into Our Identity

Write a letter to yourself affirming your God-given identity and keep it for future encouragement.

_____

_____

_____

_____

Building Deeper Connection to Faith

- Journaling Prompt: Reflect on how being fearfully and wonderfully made by God influences yourself view and actions.
- Prayer: "Lord, thank You for creating me fearfully and wonderfully. Help me to affirm my identity in You daily and live out Your purpose for my life. Amen."

Tomorrow's Journey

Today, we've discussed the importance of affirming our identity in God through the story of Esther. Reflect on how knowing you are wonderfully made can change your perspective and actions. Tomorrow, we will review the key lessons from this week and prepare for the next steps in our journey.

WEEK 1 REFLECTION

As we come to the end of Week 1, take some time to reflect on what you have learned and how it has impacted your faith journey. Use this space to jot down your thoughts, insights, and any actions you plan to take moving forward.

Reflection Questions

1. What key insights did I gain about my identity this week?

_____

_____

_____

2. How has my understanding of being a child of God changed or deepened?

_____

_____

_____

3. In what ways have I experienced God's presence and guidance during this week?

_____

_____

_____

4. What challenges did I face, and how did I overcome them?

_____

_____

_____

Personal Reflections

1. *What specific steps can I take to continue strengthening my understanding of my identity in Christ?*

_____

_____

_____

2. *How can I incorporate the lessons learned into my daily life?*

_____

_____

_____

3. *Are there any areas where I still struggle with my identity? How can I address them?*

_____

_____

_____

Action Plan

List three practical actions you will take in the coming week to nurture your understanding of your identity in Christ.

1. _____
   _____

2. _____
   _____

3. _____
   _____

PRAYER

Spend a few moments in prayer, asking God to help you integrate what you've learned into your daily life and to continue guiding you on your faith journey.

"Heavenly Father, thank You for the insights and growth I've experienced this week. Help me to carry these lessons into the coming days and to live out my identity with confidence and trust in You. Amen."

Additional Notes

Use this space to write down any additional thoughts, prayers, or reflections you have as you conclude this week.

_____

_____

_____

_____

_____

_____

Preparing for Week 2

As we move into Week 2, take a moment to prepare your heart and mind for the next steps in our journey. Review the upcoming themes and consider what you hope to learn and achieve.

Welcome to a journey of deepening faith and trust. May God bless you richly as you seek to strengthen your relationship with Him.

WEEK 2
Living Out Your Godly Identity

If you're like me, knowing something in your head is different from living it out daily. In the second week of our journey, we will delve deeper into what it means to live out our identity in Christ. This involves understanding that we are chosen, loved, and part of God's royal priesthood. We'll look at practical ways to walk in these truths daily, overcoming worldly pressures and living authentically.

This week is about moving from understanding to application. Knowing that we are chosen and loved by God is transformative. It impacts how we see ourselves, how we interact with others, and how we face life's challenges. Being part of a royal priesthood means we have a special role and responsibility in God's kingdom. We are called to live in a way that reflects His grace, love, and holiness.

We will explore practical steps to embody our godly identity, such as embracing our unique gifts, serving others with love, and standing firm in our faith amidst trials. By the end of this week, we will be equipped with tools and insights to live out our identity confidently and with purpose, recognizing that we are God's workmanship, created for good works (Ephesians 2:10).

Living out our identity in Christ isn't about perfection but about authenticity and reliance on God's grace. It's a journey of daily surrender and intentional action, allowing His truth to shape our thoughts, words, and deeds. As we navigate this week, let's commit to embracing our identity fully and courageously, trusting that God's plans for us are good and His strength is made perfect in our weakness (2 Corinthians 12:9).

Key Themes

- Chosen and Loved
- Part of a Royal Priesthood
- God's Workmanship

Anchor Scripture

"For we are God's handiwork, created in Christ Jesus to do good works, which God prepared in advance for us to do."
—*Ephesians 2:10*

Reflection

Together, let's think about the specific ways in which knowing we are chosen and loved by God can change our interactions and decisions. How can we live out our purpose as God's workmanship? Let's reflect on the roles we play in our daily lives and how we can align them with our identity in Christ.

DAY 1
REFLECTING ON GODLY ATTRIBUTES

I have to admit, I've got a bit of a bro-crush on Captain America. There, I said it. His unwavering courage, selflessness, and integrity always inspire me to be a better person. But here's the thing: I don't need a super soldier serum to develop those heroic qualities.

When I look at the Bible, Joseph's story reminds me that I can embody the same godly attributes I admire in Cap, like integrity, forgiveness, and trust in God, even when faced with incredible adversity. Joseph is like the Captain America of the Old Testament, using his gifts to save the day and inspire others.

By embracing these godly attributes that make Cap a true hero, I believe we can all unlock our own origin stories and become the heroes we were meant to be. It's not about having superpowers or a fancy shield—it's about developing character that reflects God's heart.

So while I may not be fighting aliens or HYDRA anytime soon, I can still strive to embody the heroic qualities I admire in both Captain America and biblical figures like Joseph. Are you ready to join me in this challenge?

Role Models in Scripture

Joseph, sold into slavery by his brothers, maintained his integrity and faith in God throughout his life. His story is a powerful testament to the attributes of patience, kindness, and forgiveness, reflecting God's character even in the most difficult circumstances. Joseph's journey from favored son to slave to the second most powerful man in Egypt is a remarkable story of God's providence and Joseph's steadfast faith.

Despite being wronged by his brothers and unjustly imprisoned, Joseph never wavered in his faith and integrity. His life was marked by continuous trust in God, which guided his actions and decisions. Even when faced with immense adversity, Joseph chose to honor God through his conduct. He rose to prominence in Egypt, not through deceit or manipulation, but by reflecting God's attributes in his actions. His wisdom and integrity were recognized by those around him, leading him to become Pharaoh's righthand man.

Joseph's trials were many. He faced betrayal by his own family, false accusations from Potiphar's wife, and years of imprisonment. Yet, in each situation, Joseph remained patient, trusting in God's timing and purpose. His ability to interpret dreams, a gift from God, eventually led to his rise in power. He used this position not for personal gain but to save countless lives during a severe famine. Joseph's life is a testament to how God can use our trials and talents for His greater purpose.

When Joseph finally faced his brothers, who had sold him into slavery, his response was one of grace and forgiveness. Instead of seeking revenge, he saw God's hand in his journey. Joseph's words to his brothers, *"You intended to harm me, but God intended it for good to accomplish what is now being done, the saving of many lives"* (Genesis 50:20), show his deep understanding of God's sovereignty and goodness. His ability to forgive and love those who wronged him is a powerful example of living out godly attributes.

Joseph's life demonstrates the importance of embodying godly attributes, even in adversity, and trusting that God's plans are greater than our circumstances. His story encourages us to reflect God's love, patience, and forgiveness in our own lives, trusting that He will use our trials for His glory. By maintaining our faith and integrity, we can be instruments of God's grace and providence in the world.

Scriptures to Remember

"You intended to harm me, but God intended it for good to accomplish what is now being done, the saving of many lives."
—Genesis 50:20

"And we know that in all things God works for the good of those who love him, who have been called according to his purpose."
—Romans 8:28

"But the fruit of the Spirit is love, joy, peace, forbearance, kindness, goodness, faithfulness, gentleness and self-control. Against such things there is no law."
—Galatians 5:2223

Consider This

Reflect on Joseph's journey and the godly attributes he embodied. How did his faith and integrity influence his actions and outcomes? Think about the challenges you face and how you can exhibit patience, kindness, and forgiveness in those situations. Consider how trusting in God's greater plan can change your perspective on adversity.

Questions for Reflection

1. How does Joseph's story inspire you to maintain integrity and faith in difficult circumstances?

   _____

   _____

   _____

2. What situations in your life challenge your ability to show patience, kindness, and forgiveness?

   _____

   _____

   _____

3. How can you trust that God is working through your trials for a greater purpose?

   _____

   _____

   _____

Living Into Our Identity

Identify a situation where you can practice patience, kindness, or forgiveness this week. Take a specific action to reflect God's character in that circumstance.

_____

_____

_____

_____

_____

Building Deeper Connection to Faith

- Journaling Prompt: Write about a time when you felt wronged or faced adversity. How can Joseph's response inspire you to act differently in similar situations?
- Prayer: "Heavenly Father, thank You for the example of Joseph's faith and integrity. Help me to embody patience, kindness, and forgiveness, trusting that You are working all things for good. Strengthen my faith and guide my actions so that I may reflect Your love and grace. Amen."

Tomorrow's Journey

Today, we've explored the life of Joseph and the importance of embodying godly attributes even in adversity. Reflect on how you can apply these lessons in your own life, trusting in God's greater plan. Tomorrow, we will continue to delve deeper into living out our godly identity with practical steps and insights.

DAY 2
PURPOSE IN GOD

Do you remember the first time you felt a sense of mission? For me, it was a moment of clarity amidst chaos, a realization that I was meant for something more. It was like a light bulb went off in my head, illuminating a path I hadn't seen before. This newfound mission gave me direction and a sense of fulfillment that I hadn't experienced before.

My journey to discovering my God-given mission wasn't straightforward. It involved moments of doubt, struggle, and a lot of prayer. There were times when the obstacles seemed insurmountable, and I questioned whether I was on the right path. But each time, I found strength in my faith and in the conviction that God had a purpose for me.

One of the most significant moments of clarity came during a particularly challenging period in my life. I was facing professional setbacks and personal disappointments that left me feeling lost and uncertain. In the midst of this turmoil, I turned to prayer, seeking God's guidance and purpose for my life. It was during this time of introspection and prayer that I felt a profound sense of calling. It wasn't about a specific job or role but a deeper understanding that my mission was to serve others and reflect God's love in all I do.

As I began to embrace this mission, I noticed a shift in my perspective. Challenges became opportunities to grow and serve, and setbacks were seen as part of God's refining process. This sense of mission provided a steady anchor, guiding my decisions and actions. It wasn't always easy, and there were times when I felt like giving up, but remembering that my mission was divinely inspired kept me going.

Living out my mission meant stepping out of my comfort zone and trusting God's plan, even when it didn't make sense to me. It involved taking small, faithful steps towards the vision God had placed in my heart. Each step, no matter how small, was an act of faith, trusting that God was working through me.

Role Models in Scripture

Alright, let's talk about Nehemiah the original fixer upper extraordinaire! This guy wasn't just handy with a hammer; he was a master of spiritual home improvement.

Picture this: Nehemiah's living it up as the king's cupbearer. That's like being the royal taste tester, minus the potential poisoning part. He's got a cushy job in the Persian palace, but his heart? It's back home in Jerusalem, doing backflips over the state of his beloved city.

When Nehemiah hears that Jerusalem's walls are more Swiss cheese than solid stone, something clicks. It's like God flipped on the "purpose" switch in his brain. Suddenly, our man Nehemiah isn't just passing goblets anymore he's passing on his comfortable life to answer a higher calling.

Now, convincing a king to let you leave your job to go rebuild a city? That's a tough sell. But Nehemiah pulls it off, probably with a mix of prayer and some divinely inspired persuasion skills.

Back in Jerusalem, Nehemiah faces more obstacles than a contestant on American Ninja Warrior. We're talking opposition, threats, and probably a severe lack of power tools. But does he give up?

No sir! Nehemiah's faith is stronger than his building materials. He rallies the people, organizes the work, and keeps one eye on the wall and one on the lookout for trouble.

Here's the kicker: Nehemiah's story isn't just about brick and mortar. It's about recognizing a need, stepping up to the plate (or in this case, the building site), and trusting God to provide the game plan and the resources.

Nehemiah teaches us that finding our purpose might mean stepping out of our comfort zone way out. It might mean trading in our cushy cup bearing gig for a hard hat and some calluses. But when we align our actions with God's purpose, He doesn't just cheer from the sidelines. He's right there in the trenches with us, providing strength, wisdom, and probably some much needed refreshments.

So, the next time you feel like your life's walls are crumbling, remember Nehemiah. God might be calling you to pick up a spiritual trowel and start rebuilding. Your mission, should you choose to accept it, might not involve actual walls, but it could be just as impactful.

Are you ready to be a Nehemiah in your own life? To look around, see where God's calling you to make a difference, and dive in headfirst? Trust me, with God as your project manager, there's no telling what incredible things you might build!

Scriptures to Remember

"The God of heaven will give us success. We his servants will start rebuilding…"
—Nehemiah 2:20

"I can do all this through him who gives me strength."
—Philippians 4:13

"And whatever you do, whether in word or deed, do it all in the name of the Lord Jesus, giving thanks to God the Father through him."
—Colossians 3:17

Consider This

Reflect on the moments when you felt a strong sense of mission. How did those moments shape your actions and outlook on life? Consider how embracing your God-given mission can inspire you to pursue it with determination and faith.

Questions for Reflection

1. How have you experienced a sense of mission in your life? What were the circumstances, and how did you respond?

_____

_____

_____

2. In what ways can you embrace your mission with determination and faith, trusting in God's plan?

_____

_____

_____

3. What steps can you take to seek God's guidance and strength as you fulfill your mission?

_____

_____

_____

Living Into Our Identity

Identify one area in your life where you feel God is calling you to take action. Make a plan to pursue this mission with faith and determination.

_____

_____

_____

_____

_____

Building Deeper Connection to Faith

- **Journaling Prompt**: Write about a time when you felt a clear sense of mission from God. How did it impact your faith and actions?
- **Prayer**: "Lord, thank You for the mission You have given me. Help me to pursue it with faith, courage, and determination. Guide me, strengthen me, and use me to fulfill Your purpose. Amen."

DAY 3
COMMUNITY AND SUPPORT

Have you ever felt the warmth of a supportive community? Let me tell you, it's like wrapping yourself in a cozy blanket on a chilly day. I remember a time when the encouragement and prayers of my faith community carried me through a difficult season. Everything seemed to be going sideways work challenges, strained relationships, and even my car breaking down. It was like life was playing a cosmic game of "Let's see how much we can pile on Eric."

But my faith community stepped up in ways I never expected. It wasn't just the grand gestures (like Bob offering to be my personal chauffeur), but the little things that touched my heart. Encouraging texts, surprise homecooked meals, and heartfelt prayers all made a huge difference.

During prayer meetings, I could feel the sincerity in their prayers for me. It was like each prayer was a thread, weaving a safety net that caught me when I felt like falling. Their shared wisdom gave me new perspectives, and their belief in me rekindled my own faith.

This experience showed me the power of a loving community. It's like having a team of cheerleaders, coaches, and prayer warriors all in one. Their support helped me overcome what felt insurmountable and reminded me that I'm never truly alone.

If you're going through a tough time, remember you're not alone. Look around there might be someone ready to stand by you. Or maybe you're meant to be that support for someone else.

We're all in this journey together. Sometimes we need support, sometimes we give it. There's incredible power in a community that lifts each other up and points towards God's love and purpose.

Role Models in Scripture

Ruth, a Moabite widow, found her place in the community of Israel through her loyalty and faith. Her relationship with Naomi and her integration into Naomi's community illustrate the importance of support and fellowship in our spiritual journey. Ruth's decision to stay with Naomi, saying, *"Your people will be my people and your God my God"* (Ruth 1:16), marked a significant step in her faith journey.

Ruth's journey wasn't easy. As a foreigner and a widow, she faced many challenges and uncertainties. Yet, her unwavering loyalty to Naomi and her faith in God guided her actions. Upon arriving in Bethlehem, Ruth immediately took on the task of providing for herself and Naomi by gleaning in the fields. Her diligence and hard work did not go unnoticed. Boaz, the owner of the field and a relative of Naomi, saw Ruth's dedication and extended kindness and protection to her.

Boaz's recognition of Ruth's loyalty and hard work led to a deeper relationship. He admired her for the sacrifices she made and her commitment to Naomi. Eventually, Boaz took on the role of her kinsman redeemer, marrying Ruth and securing her place in the community. Through this union, Ruth became the great-grandmother of King David, placing her in the lineage of Jesus Christ (Matthew 1:56).

Ruth's story highlights the power of community and support in finding our identity and purpose. Her relationship with Naomi and the community's acceptance demonstrates the importance of mutual support and fellowship in our spiritual growth. Ruth's example encourages us to seek and provide support within our faith communities, recognizing that we are stronger together. Her story teaches us the value of loyalty, hard work, and faith in building strong, supportive relationships within our communities.

Ruth's faithfulness and her willingness to embrace Naomi's people and God illustrate the beauty of finding our place within God's family. Her life is a testament to how God can use our circumstances, no matter how difficult, to fulfill His greater purpose. By integrating into the community and receiving their support, Ruth's life was transformed, and she became an integral part of God's plan for redemption.

Scriptures to Remember

"Your people will be my people and your God my God."
—Ruth 1:16

"But Ruth replied, 'Don't urge me to leave you or to turn back from you. Where you go I will go, and where you stay I will stay. Your people will be my people and your God my God.'"
—Ruth 1:16

"May the Lord repay you for what you have done. May you be richly rewarded by the Lord, the God of Israel, under whose wings you have come to take refuge."
—Ruth 2:12

Consider This

Reflect on Ruth's journey and the role that support and community played in her story. How can you seek out and provide support within your own faith community? Consider how loyalty, hard work, and faith can strengthen your relationships and help you find your place in God's family.

Questions for Reflection

1. How has your faith community supported you in your spiritual journey? In what ways can you provide support to others?

_____

_____

_____

2. What can you learn from Ruth's example of loyalty and hard work in your own life?

_____

_____

_____

3. How can embracing your faith community help you discover and fulfill your God-given purpose?

_____

_____

_____

Living Into Our Identity

Identify someone in your faith community who might need support and find a practical way to assist them this week.

_____

_____

_____

_____

_____

Building Deeper Connection to Faith

- Journaling Prompt: Write about a time when your faith community supported you through a difficult situation. How did that experience impact your faith and sense of belonging?
- Prayer: "Heavenly Father, thank You for the example of Ruth's loyalty and faith. Help me to be a supportive and faithful member of my community. Guide me to build strong relationships that reflect Your love and grace. Amen."

Tomorrow's Journey

Today, we've explored the importance of support and community through the story of Ruth. Reflect on how you can seek and provide support within your faith community, and how these relationships can help you grow spiritually. Tomorrow, we will delve deeper into how our identity in Christ shapes our actions and purpose in the world.

DAY 4
PRAYER AND MEDITATION

Hey there, friends. Let's talk about something we've all experienced—those days when life feels like it's coming at you faster than a caffeinated squirrel. You know what I'm talking about, right?

I remember this one day when everything was going haywire. My to-do list was longer than a CVS receipt, my phone was blowing up with notifications, and finding a quiet moment seemed about as likely as finding a unicorn in my backyard.

Now, I've got to confess something – I'm a bit of a control freak. Okay, maybe more than a bit. I'm the guy who thinks he needs to have his hands on all the levers, all the time. It's exhausting, let me tell you.

But here's the thing I've learned (and keep relearning, if I'm honest): When I finally take a deep breath, step back, and turn to God in prayer, it's like hitting a reset button on my frazzled brain.

In those moments of prayer, even if it's just a quick "Help me, God!" while I'm stuck in traffic, I'm reminded that I'm not flying solo in this crazy life. God's right there with me, probably shaking His head fondly at my attempts to do it all on my own.

It's like He's saying, "Eric, my man, slow down for a second. I've got this. How about you take a breath and actually listen for a change?"

And you know what? When I do that, when I finally quiet down and tune in to God's frequency, it's like a weight lifts off my shoulders. I remember that I don't have to have all the answers or solve all the problems. I've got a direct line to the One who does.

Role Models in Scripture

Daniel's disciplined prayer life was central to his identity and success. Despite the risk of persecution, Daniel prayed three times a day, maintaining his relationship with God. His faithfulness in prayer not only sustained him but also influenced the kings he served and demonstrated God's power.

Daniel's commitment to prayer was unwavering, even when it led to the lions' den. His consistent prayer life provided him with wisdom, courage, and favor in a foreign land. When a decree was issued forbidding prayer to anyone except the king, Daniel continued his practice of praying three times a day, as he had always done. Daniel 6:10 states, *"Now when Daniel learned that the decree had been published, he went home to his upstairs room where the windows opened toward Jerusalem. Three times a day he got down on his knees and prayed, giving thanks to his God, just as he had done before."*

Daniel's story shows us the importance of regular prayer and meditation in maintaining our identity in God. His prayers were a source of strength and guidance, helping him navigate the challenges of serving in the Babylonian and Persian empires. Even in the face of life-threatening danger, Daniel's trust in God never wavered. His faithfulness not only saved him but also revealed God's power and sovereignty to the kings and the people around him.

When Daniel was thrown into the lions' den for his unwavering faith, God protected him. Daniel 6:22 says, *"My God sent his angel, and he shut the mouths of the lions. They have not hurt me, because I was found innocent in his sight. Nor have I ever done any wrong before you, Your Majesty.*" This miraculous deliverance demonstrated the power of God and led King Darius to honor and decree reverence for the God of Daniel.

Daniel's example encourages us to prioritize prayer and meditation, trusting that these practices will deepen our relationship with God and provide the guidance we need in our daily lives. His story teaches us that maintaining a disciplined prayer life is crucial for spiritual strength and resilience. By making prayer a regular part of our routine, we can remain connected to God, receive His wisdom, and stand firm in our faith, no matter the challenges we face.

Scriptures to Remember

"Now when Daniel learned that the decree had been published, he went home to his upstairs room where the windows opened toward Jerusalem. Three times a day he got down on his knees and prayed, giving thanks to his God, just as he had done before."
—Daniel 6:10

"My God sent his angel, and he shut the mouths of the lions. They have not hurt me, because I was found innocent in his sight. Nor have I ever done any wrong before you, Your Majesty."
—Daniel 6:22

"Be joyful in hope, patient in affliction, faithful in prayer."
—Romans 12:12

Consider This

Reflect on Daniel's unwavering commitment to prayer and how it sustained him through trials. How can you incorporate regular prayer and meditation into your daily routine? Consider the impact that a disciplined prayer life can have on your spiritual strength and relationship with God.

Questions for Reflection

1. How has regular prayer or the lack of it impacted your spiritual journey?

_____

_____

_____

2. In what ways can Daniel's disciplined prayer life inspire you to deepen your own prayer practices?

_____

_____

_____

3. What challenges do you face in maintaining a regular prayer routine, and how can you overcome them?

_____

_____

_____

Living Into Our Identity

Set aside specific times each day for prayer and meditation, making it a nonnegotiable part of your routine.

_____

_____

_____

_____

_____

Building Deeper Connection to Faith

- Journaling Prompt: Write about a time when prayer sustained you through a difficult situation. How did that experience strengthen your faith and reliance on God?
- Prayer: "Heavenly Father, thank You for the example of Daniel's unwavering commitment to prayer. Help me to prioritize my prayer life and remain steadfast in my faith, trusting in Your guidance and strength. Amen."

Tomorrow's Journey

Today, we've explored the importance of a disciplined prayer life through the story of Daniel. Reflect on how you can incorporate regular prayer into your routine to strengthen your relationship with God. Tomorrow, we will delve deeper into how our identity in Christ shapes our actions and purpose in the world.

DAY 5
OVERCOMING DOUBTS

Have you ever felt like you're in way over your head? Like someone's going to tap you on the shoulder and say, "Sorry, pal, we made a mistake. You're not supposed to be here"? Well, pull up a chair, because I've got a story for you.

A while back, I landed this project at work that was about as intimidating as a grizzly bear in a tutu. I mean, on paper, it looked like it was tailormade for someone way smarter and more capable than yours truly. I felt like a kid who accidentally wandered into the adults' table at Thanksgiving dinner.

But you know what? I took a deep breath, said a quick prayer, and dove in headfirst. And let me tell you, those first few weeks? Everything that could go wrong did go wrong, and I started thinking I'd made a mistake.

But then, something crazy happened. As I kept pushing forward, little by little, things started clicking. It was like finding puzzle pieces you didn't even know were missing. Those small victories started to show up more and more frequently.

I realized all those doubts were actually pushing me to tap into strengths I didn't even know I had.

My colleagues? They were the real MVPs. Their support and encouragement were like a much-needed pit stop in a marathon I wasn't sure I could finish. I learned it's okay to lean on others—turns out, nobody expects you to be a one-man band.

Looking back now, I see it wasn't about being perfect or having all the answers. It was about being willing to take that first wobbly step, even when my knees were knocking. My faith and stubbornness (let's call it perseverance, sounds better) paid off big time. I ended up accomplishing more than I ever thought possible.

So, here's what I learned: those doubts? They're just growing pains in disguise. Sometimes, the most important thing is to keep putting one foot in front of the other, even if you're not sure where the path is leading. Trust me, you might surprise yourself with where you end up!

Role Models in Scripture

Have you ever looked at Gideon's story in the Bible? Now there's a guy who really felt in over his head!

In the book of Judges, we find Gideon threshing wheat in a winepress, trying to hide from the Midianites. That's when an angel of the Lord shows up and says, *"The Lord is with you, mighty warrior"* (Judges 6:12). Can you imagine Gideon's reaction? He probably looked around thinking, "Who, me? Mighty warrior? There must be some mistake."

Gideon's response is so relatable. He says, *"But Lord, how can I save Israel? My clan is the weakest in Manasseh, and I am the least in my family"* (Judges 6:15). It's like he's echoing every doubt I had when I started that challenging project at work.

But here's where it gets interesting. God doesn't give up on Gideon. Instead, He patiently reassures him, saying, *"I will be with you, and you will strike down all the Midianites"* (Judges 6:16). It's not about Gideon's strength, but God's.

As Gideon steps out in faith, albeit with some divine prodding and a few fleece tests, amazing things start to happen. He goes from hiding in a winepress to leading an army of 300 men against thousands of Midianites—and winning!

What strikes me about Gideon's story is how God uses his doubts to build his faith. Every time Gideon hesitates, God provides another sign, another reassurance. It reminds me of how, in my own experience, pushing through doubts led me to discover strengths I didn't know I had.

The Bible tells us, *"The Lord turned to him and said, 'Go in the strength you have and save Israel out of Midian's hand. Am I not sending you?'"* (Judges 6:14). This verse always encourages me. It's like God's saying, "I've got this, and I've got you."

So, here's what I take from Gideon's story and my own experience: Doubt isn't the enemy of faith—it can actually be the springboard. When we face our doubts honestly and bring them to God, amazing things can happen. It's not about having it all together or feeling super confident. It's about being willing to take that first step, even when your knees are shaking.

Remember, God doesn't call the qualified; He qualifies the called. So the next time you're feeling like you're not up to the task, remember Gideon. Remember that guy who felt way out of his league but ended up leading his people to victory. And maybe, just maybe, take that first step of faith. You might be surprised where it leads you.

Scriptures to Remember

"The Lord is with you, mighty warrior."
—Judges 6:12

*"But Lord," Gideon asked, "how can I save Israel? My
clan is the weakest in Manasseh, and I am the least in my
family."*
—Judges 6:15

*"I will be with you, and you will strike down all the
Midianites, leaving none alive."*
—Judges 6:16

*"The Lord turned to him and said, 'Go in the strength
you have and save Israel out of Midian's hand. Am I not
sending you?'"*
—Judges 6:14

Consider This

Reflect on Gideon's journey and the role that doubt and
reassurance played in his story. How can you bring your doubts to God
and allow Him to turn them into strengths? Consider the challenges
you face and how stepping out in faith can lead to unexpected victories.

Questions for Reflection

1. How have you experienced doubt in your faith journey, and how did you respond?

_____

_____

_____

2. In what ways can Gideon's story inspire you to step out in faith despite your doubts?

_____

_____

_____

3. What steps can you take to trust God's calling and move forward in faith, even when you feel unqualified?

_____

_____

_____

Living Into Our Identity

Identify a situation where you feel inadequate or doubtful. Bring this situation to God in prayer, asking for His reassurance and guidance.

_____

_____

_____

_____

_____

Building Deeper Connection to Faith

- Journaling Prompt: Write about a time when you felt doubt but chose to step out in faith. How did God show up in that situation?
- Prayer: "Heavenly Father, thank You for the example of Gideon's faith journey. Help me to bring my doubts to You and trust in Your strength and guidance. Give me the courage to take the first step of faith, knowing that You are with me. Amen."

Tomorrow's Journey

Today, we've explored the importance of facing our doubts and stepping out in faith through the story of Gideon. Reflect on how you can bring your doubts to God and trust Him to qualify you for the tasks He has called you to. Tomorrow, we will continue to delve deeper into living out our identity in Christ with practical steps and insights.

WEEK 2 REFLECTION

As we come to the end of Week 2, take some time to reflect on what you have learned and how it has impacted your journey of discovering your identity in Christ. Use this space to jot down your thoughts, insights, and any actions you plan to take moving forward.

Reflection Questions

1. *What key insights did I gain about my identity in Christ this week?*

_____

_____

_____

2. *How has my understanding of being a child of God changed or deepened?*

_____

_____

_____

3. *In what ways have I experienced God's love and affirmation during this week?*

_____

_____

_____

4. *What challenges did I face, and how did I overcome them?*

_____

_____

_____

Personal Reflections

1. *What specific steps can I take to continue embracing my identity in Christ?*

_____

_____

_____

2. *How can I incorporate the lessons learned into my daily life?*

_____

_____

_____

3. *Are there any areas where I still struggle with my identity? How can I address them?*

_____

_____

_____

Action Plan

List three practical actions you will take in the coming week to nurture your identity in Christ.

1. _____
   _____

2. _____
   _____

3. _____
   _____

PRAYER

Spend a few moments in prayer, asking God to help you integrate what you've learned into your daily life and to continue guiding you on your journey of discovering your true identity.

"Heavenly Father, thank You for the insights and growth I've experienced this week. Help me to carry these lessons into the coming days and to live out my identity in Christ with confidence and trust in You. Amen."

Additional Notes

Use this space to write down any additional thoughts, prayers, or reflections you have as you conclude this week.

_____

_____

_____

_____

_____

_____

_____

_____

Preparing for Week 3

Alright, folks, let's gear up for Week 3! As we dive deeper into our identity adventure, take a moment to prepare your heart and mind. Think about what you've learned so far and what you're hoping to discover next.

This journey isn't just about learning facts it's about transformation. We're on a path to discovering our true identity in Christ, and trust me, it's a gamechanger.

Consider the upcoming themes and what you hope to achieve. Are you looking to shed old labels? Hoping to understand God's purpose for you better? Bring those hopes and questions to God.

Remember, you're exactly where you need to be. God's got big plans for you, and He's excited to reveal more of who He created you to be.

Welcome to the next phase of "Identity: Discovering Who You Are." May God bless you richly as you seek to embrace who you are in Him. Ready? Let's do this!

WEEK 3
Embracing Your Role as a Leader and Light

As we head into the final week of our journey, I want to talk about something that might make some of us a bit uncomfortable: being leaders and lights in the world. Now, if you're anything like me, the idea of being a "leader" might make you want to hide under your bed. But here's the thing God's idea of leadership isn't about being perfect or having all the answers.

This week, we're going to explore what it really means to be a leader in God's kingdom. Spoiler alert: it's more about serving others and reflecting Christ's love than it is about being in charge. We'll look at how we can set an example for others, not by being flawless, but by being authentic in our faith journey.

We'll also dive into what Jesus meant when He called us the "light of the world." Don't worry, it doesn't involve wearing a lighthouse costume (though that would be pretty funny). It's about letting God's love shine through us in our everyday lives.

And here's the best part we'll be reminded that we're God's beloved. That's right, the Creator of the universe cherishes you. How amazing is that?

By the end of this week, my hope is that we'll all feel a bit more confident in our identity in Christ. Not because we've suddenly become super Christians, but because we've realized that God can use us, quirks and all, to make a difference in the world.

So, are you ready to embrace your role as a leader and a light? Don't worry, we're in this together. Let's see what God has in store for us!

Key Themes

- A Leader of Men
- The Light of the World
- His Beloved

Anchor Scripture

"You are the light of the world. A town built on a hill cannot be hidden."
—*Matthew 5:14*

Reflection

Let's think about this: How can we be a light in our community? I'm talking simple stuff maybe a kind word to a stressed-out cashier or helping a neighbor with their groceries. And here's a mindblower: we're God's beloved. How does knowing that change things for you? Let's consider how this amazing truth can help us inspire others, even on our not-so-great days. Who knows what God might do through us when we embrace who He says we are?

DAY 1
DAILY PRACTICES

You know, it's funny how the little things can make such a big difference, isn't it? Take my mornings, for example. I used to roll out of bed, grab my phone, and immediately start scrolling through emails or social media. Talk about starting the day stressed!

But then I decided to try something different. I started setting aside just a few minutes each morning for prayer and reflection. Nothing fancy, mind you sometimes it's just a quick "Hey God, help me not to mess up too badly today!" But let me tell you, it's been a gamechanger.

It's like hitting a reset button on my brain before the day even starts. When I take that moment to connect with God, it's as if everything comes into focus. Suddenly, I'm not just rushing through my day I've got a sense of purpose, a reminder of what really matters.

And here's the thing: it's not about being perfect or super spiritual. It's just about showing up and being open to what God might want to say. Sometimes it's a profound insight, sometimes it's just a feeling of peace. Either way, it sets the tone for my whole day.

I've found that these little habits whether it's prayer, reading a Bible verse, or just sitting in silence for a minute they're like anchors in the storm of life. They keep me grounded when things get crazy (which, let's face it, is pretty much every day).

So, if you're feeling overwhelmed or disconnected, why not give it a try? Start small even just a minute or two can make a difference. You might be surprised at how these little moments with God can transform your day-to-day life. Trust me, if I can do it, anyone can!

Role Models in Scripture

Jesus often withdrew to lonely places to pray, spent time teaching His disciples, and served those around Him with compassion and love. His life on earth was marked by a rhythm of prayer, teaching, and service. He regularly spent time in solitude with God, teaching His disciples, and ministering to the needs of the people.

These daily practices not only sustained Jesus but also equipped Him to fulfill His mission. His example shows us the importance of establishing daily habits that nurture our relationship with God and enable us to live out our identity in Christ. Jesus' practices of prayer, study, and service encourage us to create a daily routine that prioritizes our spiritual growth and equips us to serve others with love and compassion.

Jesus' commitment to prayer was evident throughout His ministry. Luke 5:16 tells us, *"But Jesus often withdrew to lonely places and prayed."* These times of solitude allowed Him to connect deeply with the Father, drawing strength and guidance for His ministry. Jesus' prayers were a source of sustenance and direction, enabling Him to stay aligned with God's will.

In addition to prayer, Jesus dedicated significant time to teaching His disciples. He imparted wisdom, corrected misunderstandings, and prepared them for their future mission. This teaching was not just about imparting knowledge but about shaping their character and faith. Matthew 5:12 describes how Jesus taught His disciples: *"Now when Jesus saw the crowds, he went up on a mountainside and sat down. His disciples came to him, and he began to teach them."*

Jesus also served those around Him with compassion and love. He healed the sick, fed the hungry, and comforted the brokenhearted. His acts of service were tangible expressions of God's love and mercy. Mark 10:45 states, *"For even the Son of Man did not come to be served, but to serve, and to give his life as a ransom for many."*

These three practices—prayer, teaching, and service—were integral to Jesus' life and ministry. They sustained Him and enabled Him to fulfill His mission on earth. By following His example, we can establish daily habits that strengthen our relationship with God and empower us to serve others.

Scriptures to Remember

"But Jesus often withdrew to lonely places and prayed."
—Luke 5:16

"Now when Jesus saw the crowds, he went up on a mountainside and sat down. His disciples came to him, and he began to teach them."
—Matthew 5:12

"For even the Son of Man did not come to be served, but to serve, and to give his life as a ransom for many."
—Mark 10:45

Consider This

Reflect on Jesus' daily practices of prayer, teaching, and service. How can you incorporate these habits into your own life? Consider the impact that regular prayer, study of God's Word, and acts of service can have on your spiritual growth and your ability to live out your identity in Christ.

Questions for Reflection

1. How can you create a daily routine that includes prayer, study, and service?

   _____

   _____

   _____

2. In what ways can Jesus' example of teaching and serving inspire you to support and uplift others?

   _____

   _____

   _____

3. What specific steps can you take to deepen your relationship with God through regular prayer and solitude?

   _____

   _____

   _____

Living Into Our Identity

Identify one new habit you can incorporate into your daily routine that will help you grow spiritually and serve others more effectively.

_____

_____

_____

_____

_____

Building Deeper Connection to Faith

- Journaling Prompt: Write about how you can follow Jesus' example of balancing prayer, teaching, and service in your daily life.
- Prayer: "Lord, thank You for the example of Jesus' life. Help me to establish daily habits of prayer, study, and service that will draw me closer to You and equip me to serve others with love and compassion. Amen."

Tomorrow's Journey

Today, we've explored the importance of establishing daily habits that nurture our relationship with God and enable us to live out our identity in Christ, following the example of Jesus. Reflect on how you can incorporate prayer, teaching, and service into your daily routine. Tomorrow, we will continue to delve deeper into living out our identity in Christ with practical steps and insights.

DAY 2
SERVING OTHERS

You know, it's funny how the smallest things can sometimes hit you like a ton of bricks in a good way, I mean. I remember this one day when I was feeling about as useful as a screen door on a submarine. Everything was going wrong, and I was convinced I was invisible to the entire world.

Then, out of nowhere, a friend of mine walks up. Now, he didn't solve world hunger or anything. He just smiled, put his hand on my shoulder, and said, "Hey, you're doing great. Hang in there." That's it. But let me tell you, in that moment, it was like someone had flipped a switch inside me.

It got me thinking about how we never really know what's going on in someone else's world, you know? That person who cut you off in traffic? Maybe they just lost their job. The cashier who seems grumpy? Could be dealing with a sick kid at home.

And here's the kicker we have the power to be that person who makes someone's day better. It doesn't take much. A smile, a kind word, holding the door open for someone whose arms are full of groceries. These little acts of kindness, they're like pebbles thrown into a pond. The ripples go way further than we can see.

I think that's what Jesus was talking about when He said to love our neighbors. It's not always about grand gestures. Sometimes it's just about being present and kind in the small moments.

So, next time you're out and about, why not try spreading a little kindness? You never know your small act might be exactly what someone needs to turn their whole day around. And hey, it might just make your day better too!

Role Models in Scripture

In the parable of the Good Samaritan, Jesus describes a man who goes out of his way to help a stranger in need. This parable is one of the most profound teachings of Jesus, illustrating the essence of loving our neighbor as ourselves. The story begins with a man traveling from Jerusalem to Jericho who is attacked by robbers, stripped of his clothes, beaten, and left halfdead. A priest and a Levite, both respected figures in Jewish society, pass by the injured man without offering any help. Their actions, or lack thereof, highlight the indifference and neglect that can sometimes characterize even those who are supposed to embody godliness.

Then comes a Samaritan, a member of a group despised and looked down upon by the Jews. Despite cultural and religious animosities, the Samaritan shows profound compassion and mercy. He tends to the injured man's wounds, pouring on oil and wine, and then places him on his own donkey to take him to an inn where he can recover. The Samaritan not only provides immediate care but also ensures ongoing support by paying the innkeeper and promising to cover any additional expenses.

This parable illustrates the importance of serving others selflessly and seeing every person as our neighbor, regardless of societal boundaries. The Samaritan's actions reflect the kind of love and service that Jesus calls us to embody in our daily lives. By choosing to help the wounded man, the Samaritan demonstrates that true neighborly love transcends ethnic, religious, and social barriers. His example challenges us to look beyond our prejudices and to serve those in need with genuine compassion and generosity.

The Good Samaritan's story is a powerful reminder that our identity in Christ compels us to act with love and kindness towards all people, especially those who are vulnerable and in need. It calls us to step out of our comfort zones, to offer help without hesitation, and to make personal sacrifices for the wellbeing of others. This level of service reflects the heart of God and shows the world the transformative power of His love.

Scriptures to Remember

"But a Samaritan, as he traveled, came where the man was; and when he saw him, he took pity on him."
—Luke 10:33

"Which of these three do you think was a neighbor to the man who fell into the hands of robbers? The expert in the law replied, 'The one who had mercy on him.' Jesus told him, 'Go and do likewise.'"
—Luke 10:3637

"Love your neighbor as yourself."
—Mark 12:31

Consider This

Reflect on the actions of the Good Samaritan and how they demonstrate true neighborly love. How can you embody this kind of selfless service in your daily life? Consider the barriers that may prevent you from helping others and how you can overcome them to live out your identity in Christ.

Questions for Reflection

1. How can you show compassion and mercy to those in need, regardless of their background or circumstances?

_____

_____

_____

2. In what ways does the story of the Good Samaritan challenge you to step out of your comfort zone and serve others selflessly?

_____

_____

_____

3. What personal sacrifices can you make to help someone in need this week?

_____

_____

_____

Living Into Our Identity

Identify someone in your community who needs help and make a plan to assist them, whether through a kind act, financial support, or offering your time.

_____

_____

_____

_____

_____

Building Deeper Connection to Faith

- Journaling Prompt: Write about a time when you received help from someone unexpectedly. How did that experience impact you, and how can you pay it forward?
- Prayer: "Lord, thank You for the example of the Good Samaritan. Help me to see every person as my neighbor and to serve others with compassion and love. Give me the courage to step out of my comfort zone and to make personal sacrifices for the wellbeing of those in need. Amen."

Tomorrow's Journey

Today, we've explored the importance of selfless service through the parable of the Good Samaritan. Reflect on how you can embody this kind of love and compassion in your daily life. Tomorrow, we will continue to delve deeper into living out our identity in Christ with practical steps and insights.

DAY 3
RESILIENCE AND FAITH

Man, have I ever been there. Let me tell you about a time when my faith was stretched thinner than my old college t-shirt.

It was a few years back when everything decided to go sideways at once. I'm talking job loss, health issues, and family drama the whole nine yards. It felt like I was trying to juggle flaming torches while riding a unicycle. Backwards. On a tightrope.

There were days when I'd look up at the sky and think, "God, are You sure You've got the right guy here? Because this feels like a cosmic mix-up." My faith, which I thought was pretty solid, suddenly felt about as stable as a Jenga tower in an earthquake.

But here's the thing it was in those moments, when I was hanging on by my fingernails, that I learned what faith really means. It's not about having all the answers or feeling super spiritual. Sometimes, it's just about taking the next step, even when you can't see the whole staircase.

Looking back now, I can see how those tough times were like spiritual boot camp. They stripped away all the fluff and forced me to really wrestle with what I believed. And you know what? My faith came out stronger on the other side. Not because I'm some perfect Christian, mind you, but because I learned that God is faithful even when everything else is falling apart.

These experiences taught me that trusting God isn't always easy or comfortable. Sometimes it's messy and scary. But it's in those moments, when we choose to trust even though we're scared out of our minds, that our faith grows in ways we never expected.

So, if you're in one of those seasons right now, hang in there. Your faith might feel wobbly but remember even wobbly faith can move mountains. And who knows? You might just come out the other side with a faith that's stronger and deeper than you ever imagined.

Role Models in Scripture

Job, who faced immense suffering, remained faithful to God despite losing everything. His resilience and unwavering faith are powerful examples of trusting God in the midst of trials. Job's life was marked by great prosperity and severe testing. Despite losing his wealth, health, and children, Job refused to curse God. His profound declaration, *"Though He slay me, yet will I hope in Him"* (Job 13:15), reflects his deep trust in God's sovereignty and goodness.

Job's friends questioned his faith, but Job's resilience came from his unshakable belief in God's character. His story encourages us to hold onto our faith in God, even when we don't understand our circumstances. Job's resilience teaches us that our identity in God provides the strength to endure and that God's purposes and goodness prevail, even in suffering.

Throughout his trials, Job never wavered in his commitment to God. He questioned and lamented, but he always turned to God in his pain and confusion. Job 1:21 records Job's response to his losses: *"The Lord gave and the Lord has taken away; may the name of the Lord be praised."* This response underscores Job's recognition of God's ultimate authority and his willingness to submit to God's will, even in the face of profound loss.

Job's faith was further tested by his friends, who insisted that his suffering was a result of his sin. Despite their accusations and the additional burden of defending his integrity, Job remained steadfast. He maintained his innocence and continued to seek understanding from God. Job's perseverance in faith, even when his friends turned against him, exemplifies a deep-rooted trust in God that transcends human understanding.

In the end, God vindicated Job, restoring his fortunes and blessing him with even greater prosperity than before. Job 42:10 states, *"After Job had prayed for his friends, the Lord restored his fortunes and gave him twice as much as he had before."* Job's restoration highlights God's faithfulness and the reward of enduring faith.

Scriptures to Remember

"Though He slay me, yet will I hope in Him."
—Job 13:15

"The Lord gave and the Lord has taken away; may the name of the Lord be praised."
—Job 1:21

"After Job had prayed for his friends, the Lord restored his fortunes and gave him twice as much as he had before."
—Job 42:10

Consider This

Reflect on Job's unwavering faith in the face of immense suffering. How can you hold onto your faith in God during your own trials? Consider how Job's trust in God's character can inspire you to remain steadfast, even when you don't understand your circumstances.

Questions for Reflection

1. How has suffering or trials challenged your faith, and how have you responded?

_____

_____

_____

2. In what ways can Job's story encourage you to trust in God's sovereignty and goodness, even in difficult times?

_____

_____

_____

3. What steps can you take to deepen your trust in God, especially when facing adversity?

_____

_____

_____

Living Into Our Identity

Identify a challenging situation in your life and make a conscious effort to trust God's plan and goodness, even if you don't understand why it's happening.

_____

_____

_____

_____

_____

Building Deeper Connection to Faith

- Journaling Prompt: Write about a time when you faced significant trials and how your faith in God helped you endure. Reflect on what you learned about God's character through that experience.
- Prayer: "Lord, thank You for the example of Job's unwavering faith. Help me to trust in Your sovereignty and goodness, even in the midst of trials. Strengthen my faith and help me to endure with hope and perseverance. Amen."

Tomorrow's Journey

Today, we've explored the importance of maintaining faith and trust in God through the story of Job. Reflect on how you can remain steadfast in your faith, even during difficult times. Tomorrow, we will continue to delve deeper into living out our identity in Christ with practical steps and insights.

DAY 4
SHARING YOUR FAITH

Have you ever felt a nudge to share your faith but hesitated? I sure have. There was this time I was chatting with a friend who was clearly going through a tough patch. I felt that inner prompting to offer some words of encouragement, to share how my faith helps me through hard times. But I froze up. It's like my brain and my mouth suddenly lost connection.

It's a tricky balance, isn't it? We want to be a light in the world, to offer hope when things seem dark. But then there's that worry about how it'll be received. Will they think I'm being preachy? What if I say the wrong thing?

Looking back, I realize those small moments can make a big difference. Sharing our faith doesn't always mean giving a sermon on a street corner. Sometimes it's just being there, offering a kind word, or sharing a bit of our own journey when the moment feels right.

I've learned that it's okay to feel nervous about these things. The important part is being willing to step out in faith when we feel that nudge. We don't have to have all the answers. We just need to be open to how God might use us to bring a little hope into someone's day.

So next time you feel that prompting, why not take a deep breath and go for it? You never know your words might be exactly what someone needs to hear.

Role Models in Scripture

Paul, formerly known as Saul, was a fervent persecutor of Christians until his dramatic conversion on the road to Damascus. After encountering Christ, Paul became one of the most passionate and effective evangelists in history. His letters and missionary journeys helped establish the early Church and spread the gospel far and wide.

Paul's commitment to sharing his faith was unwavering, even in the face of imprisonment, beatings, and shipwrecks. He wrote, "*I am not ashamed of the gospel, because it is the power of God that brings salvation to everyone who believes*" (Romans 1:16). Paul's dedication to his mission reminds us that sharing our faith is a vital part of living out our identity in Christ. His example encourages us to boldly share the gospel, knowing that it has the power to transform lives.

Paul's journey wasn't without challenges. He faced intense opposition and persecution, yet his resolve never faltered. He traveled extensively, preaching the gospel and establishing churches, often under dire circumstances. Acts 9:1516 records God's words about Paul's mission: "*But the Lord said to Ananias, 'Go! This man is my chosen instrument to proclaim my name to the Gentiles and their kings and to the people of Israel. I will show him how much he must suffer for my name.'*" Paul embraced this calling with fervor and dedication, fully aware of the trials he would face.

His letters to the early churches are filled with encouragement, instruction, and exhortation, showing his deep concern for their spiritual growth and unity. In 2 Timothy 4:7, Paul reflects on his journey: "*I have fought the good fight, I have finished the race, I have kept the faith.*" His life exemplifies perseverance, faithfulness, and an unyielding commitment to God's mission.

Scriptures to Remember

"I am not ashamed of the gospel, because it is the power of God that brings salvation to everyone who believes."
—Romans 1:16

"You are the light of the world. A town built on a hill cannot be hidden. Neither do people light a lamp and put it under a bowl. Instead they put it on its stand, and it gives light to everyone in the house. In the same way, let your light shine before others, that they may see your good deeds and glorify your Father in heaven."
—Matthew 5:1416

"But in your hearts revere Christ as Lord. Always be prepared to give an answer to everyone who asks you to give the reason for the hope that you have. But do this with gentleness and respect."
—1 Peter 3:15

"But you will receive power when the Holy Spirit comes on you; and you will be my witnesses in Jerusalem, and in all Judea and Samaria, and to the ends of the earth."
—Acts 1:8

Consider This

Reflect on being the light of the world and sharing the gospel. How can you embody Paul's dedication and courage in sharing your faith? Spend time journaling about how you can be a light in your community and how you can seize opportunities to share the hope you have in Christ.

Questions for Reflection

1. How can you be a light in your community?

_____

_____

_____

2. What opportunities do you have to share your faith with others?

_____

_____

_____

3. How can you embody Paul's dedication and courage in sharing your faith?

_____

_____

_____

Living Into Our Identity

Share your testimony with someone or invite them to a church event.

_____

_____

_____

_____

_____

Building Deeper Connection to Faith

- **Journaling Prompt**: Reflect on opportunities you have to share your faith and how you can be a light in your community.
- **Prayer**: "Lord, help me to be a light in my community and share the hope I have in You. Give me the courage to share my faith with others. Amen."

DAY 5
FINAL REFLECTION AND COMMITMENT

Have you ever felt like you're in a spiritual waiting room? I sure have. There was this season in my life where everything felt uncertain. I was waiting for answers, for direction, for... well, anything really. It was like being stuck in a fog, unable to see the road ahead.

During that time, I found myself clinging to God's promises like a life raft in choppy waters. I'd read verses about God's plans for our future, His faithfulness, His love and I'd think, "Okay, God, I'm holding You to this."

Let me tell you, it wasn't always pretty. There were days when doubt crept in like an unwelcome houseguest. I'd catch myself wondering, "Am I just fooling myself? Is anything going to change?"

But here's what I learned: commitment to God's promises isn't about feeling 100% certain all the time. It's about choosing to trust even when our emotions are all over the place. It's about taking that next step forward, even when we can't see where it's leading.

Looking back now, I can see how that season of waiting shaped my faith. It taught me to rely on God's faithfulness rather than my own understanding. And you know what? That's a lesson I'm still learning every day.

So if you're in a season of uncertainty right now, hang in there. Keep holding onto those promises. Your faith might feel shaky, but remember even a mustard seed of faith can move mountains. Trust that God's timing is perfect, even when it doesn't match our schedules. Who knows? This season of waiting might just be preparing you for something amazing ahead.

Role Models in Scripture

Abraham, the father of faith, demonstrated unwavering commitment to God's promises. His willingness to leave his homeland and trust God's direction shows the importance of commitment in our spiritual journey. Abraham's life was marked by radical obedience and faith. When God called him to leave his country and go to a land He would show him, Abraham obeyed without hesitation. Genesis 12:14 recounts God's call and Abraham's immediate response: *"The Lord had said to Abram, 'Go from your country, your people and your father's household to the land I will show you. I will make you into a great nation, and I will bless you; I will make your name great, and you will be a blessing."* So Abraham went, as the Lord had told him.

Abraham's faith journey was not without its challenges. One of the most significant tests was the long wait for the promised son, Isaac. Despite their advanced age and Sarah's initial disbelief, Abraham believed in God's promise. Hebrews 11:1112 highlights this faith: *"And by faith even Sarah, who was past childbearing age, was enabled to bear children because she considered him faithful who had made the promise. And so from this one man, and he as good as dead, came descendants as numerous as the stars in the sky and as countless as the sand on the seashore."*

Another profound challenge was when God tested Abraham's willingness to sacrifice Isaac. This test of faith is captured in Genesis 22:12: *"Some time later God tested Abraham. He said to him, 'Abraham!' 'Here I am,' he replied. Then God said, 'Take your son, your only son, whom you love—Isaac—and go to the region of Moriah. Sacrifice him there as a burnt offering on a mountain I will show you."* Abraham's immediate obedience and trust in God's provision were remarkable. As he prepared to sacrifice Isaac, God intervened, providing a ram as a substitute offering (Genesis 22:1213).

Abraham's unwavering commitment to God's promises, despite not seeing them fulfilled immediately, teaches us the value of steadfast faith. His life encourages us to reflect on our commitment to God and renew our dedication to living out our identity in Him. Romans 4:2021 reflects on Abraham's faith: *"Yet he did not waver through unbelief regarding the promise of God, but was strengthened in his faith and gave glory to God, being fully persuaded that God had power to do what he had promised."*

Abraham's story inspires us to trust God's timing and remain faithful, knowing that He is faithful to His promises. Abraham's faith was not just in the promises but in the Promise Giver. This deep trust allowed him to navigate uncertainties and challenges with confidence in God's ultimate plan. His journey of faith is a testament to the power of believing in God's faithfulness, even when the fulfillment of His promises seems distant.

Scriptures to Remember

"Since, then, you have been raised with Christ, set your hearts on things above, where Christ is, seated at the right hand of God. Set your minds on things above, not on

earthly things. For you died, and your life is now hidden with Christ in God."
—Colossians 3:13

"Brothers and sisters, I do not consider myself yet to have taken hold of it. But one thing I do: Forgetting what is behind and straining toward what is ahead, I press on toward the goal to win the prize for which God has called me heavenward in Christ Jesus."
—Philippians 3:1314

"I have fought the good fight, I have finished the race, I have kept the faith."
—2 Timothy 4:7

Consider This

Reflect on setting your heart on things above and committing to a godly identity. How can you embody Abraham's unwavering commitment to God's promises? Spend time journaling about the changes you will make to fully embrace a godly identity and how you can stay committed to this path.

Questions for Reflection

1. What changes will you make to fully embrace a godly identity?

_____

_____

_____

2. How can you stay committed to this path?

_____

_____

_____

3. What steps can you take to strengthen your faith and trust in God's promises?

_____

_____

_____

Living Into Our Identity

Write a commitment statement to live out your godly identity and share it with a trusted friend or mentor for accountability.

_____

_____

_____

_____

_____

Building Deeper Connection to Faith

- Journaling Prompt: Reflect on the changes you will make to fully embrace a godly identity and how you can stay committed.
- Prayer: "Lord, help me to stay committed to living out my godly identity. Strengthen my faith and guide my steps as I follow You. Amen."

Tomorrow's Journey

Today, we've reflected on the importance of commitment to God's promises through the example of Abraham. As we conclude this week, let's reflect on how we can stay committed to living out our godly identity.

WEEK 3 REFLECTION

As we come to the end of Week 3, take some time to reflect on what you have learned and how it has impacted your journey of discovering your identity in Christ. Use the provided space to jot down your thoughts, insights, and any actions you plan to take moving forward.

Reflection Questions

1. What key insights did I gain about my identity in Christ this week?

_____

_____

_____

2. How has my understanding of being God's workmanship and a new creation changed or deepened?

_____

_____

_____

3. In what ways have I experienced God's love and affirmation during this week?

_____

_____

_____

4. What challenges did I face, and how did I overcome them?

_____

_____

_____

Personal Reflections

1. What specific steps can I take to continue embracing my identity in Christ?

_____

_____

_____

2. How can I incorporate the lessons learned into my daily life?

_____

_____

_____

3. Are there any areas where I still struggle with my identity? How can I address them?

_____

_____

_____

Action Plan

List three practical actions you will take in the coming week to nurture your identity in Christ.

1. _____
   _____

2. _____
   _____

3. _____
   _____

PRAYER

Spend a few moments in prayer, asking God to help you integrate what you've learned into your daily life and to continue guiding you on your journey of discovering your true identity.

"Heavenly Father, thank You for the insights and growth I've experienced this week. Help me to carry these lessons into the coming days and to live out my identity in Christ with confidence and trust in You. Amen."

Additional Notes

Use this space to write down any additional thoughts, prayers, or reflections you have as you conclude this week.

_____

_____

_____

_____

_____

_____

_____

_____

Preparing for the Future

As we conclude this devotional journey, take a moment to reflect on how far you have come and to prepare your heart and mind for continuing to grow in faith. Consider what you hope to achieve and how you will continue to seek God's guidance and strength.

Welcome to a lifetime of deepening faith and trust. May God bless you richly as you continue to strengthen your relationship with Him.

Embracing Your Identity Daily

Understanding your identity in Christ is not a onetime event but a continuous process of growth and renewal. Each day presents an opportunity to reaffirm who you are in Him and to live out that truth in your daily life. Here are some practical steps to help you continue this journey:

1. Daily Reflection and Prayer: Set aside time each day to reflect on your identity in Christ. Pray for strength and guidance to live out this truth in every aspect of your life.
2. Scripture Engagement: Keep God's Word at the forefront of your mind. Memorize key verses that affirm your identity and meditate on them regularly. Let these truths shape your thoughts and actions.
3. Community Support: Surround yourself with a community of believers who can support and encourage you. Share your journey with others and allow them to speak truth into your life. Engage in discussions, attend small groups, and build meaningful relationships.

4. Practical Application: Look for ways to apply what you've learned in your everyday life. Whether it's through acts of service, showing love and kindness, or making godly decisions, let your identity in Christ guide your actions.

Continuing the Journey

As you move forward, remember that this journey of discovering your identity in Christ is ongoing. There will be challenges and moments of doubt, but God's truth remains steadfast. Lean on Him, trust in His promises, and continue to seek His guidance.

Your identity in Christ is the foundation of your faith and daily living. Each day presents a new opportunity to grow deeper in your understanding of who you are in Him. It's important to remember that this process is not about perfection, but about progress and perseverance. Embrace the journey, knowing that God is with you every step of the way.

Reflect on the key truths you've learned over these past weeks:

1. God's Unchanging Love: Remember that your identity is rooted in God's unwavering love for you. He created you, knows you intimately, and loves you unconditionally. This love is the bedrock of your identity, providing you with a sense of worth and belonging.
2. New Creation in Christ: Embrace the transformation that comes from being a new creation in Christ. The old has gone, and the new is here. This new identity empowers you to live differently, with a renewed mind and heart aligned with God's will.

3. God's Workmanship: You are God's handiwork, created for good works. This means that your life has purpose and significance. God has prepared good works for you to do, and as you walk in your identity, you will fulfill the unique calling He has placed on your life.

4. Resilience in Trials: Understand that your identity in Christ gives you strength to endure trials and challenges. Like Abraham, Joseph, and Job, your faith will be tested, but it will also be strengthened. Trust in God's faithfulness and His ability to work all things for your good.

Embrace the Lifelong Journey

Understand that discovering and embracing your identity in Christ is a lifelong journey. There will be highs and lows, but each moment is an opportunity to grow closer to God. Lean into His promises and let His truth shape your life. Remember, the journey is not about arriving at a destination, but about continuously walking with God and becoming more like Christ.

As you continue on this journey, be encouraged by the truth that you are deeply loved, uniquely created, and called for a purpose. Trust in God's promises, rely on His strength, and keep moving forward in faith. Your identity in Christ is a precious gift, and as you embrace it, you will experience the fullness of life that God intends for you.

> *"Trust in the Lord with all your heart and lean not on your own understanding; in all your ways submit to him, and he will make your paths straight."*
> —Proverbs 3:56

PRAYER FOR IDENTITY
Discovering Who You Are

Opening:

> *"Heavenly Father, I come before You with a humble heart, recognizing Your greatness and love for me."*

Thanksgiving:

> *"Thank You, Lord, for guiding me through this journey of discovering my true identity in You. I am grateful for the wisdom and insights You have provided."*

Reflection:

> *"Lord, I have learned that my true identity is found in being Your child, created in Your image, and called to live out the fruits of the Spirit. I understand the importance of community, prayer, and resilience in maintaining my godly identity."*

Petitions:

> *"Father, I ask for Your strength and guidance as I continue to embrace my godly identity. Help me to resist*

worldly influences and remain steadfast in my faith. Fill
me with Your Spirit so that I may reflect Your love and
light in all I do."

Commitment:

> *"I commit to living out my identity in Christ each day,*
> *making decisions that honor You and seeking to serve*
> *others as Jesus did. Help me to stay rooted in Your Word*
> *and connected with my faith community."*

Intercession:

> *"I also lift up those who are struggling with their identity.*
> *May they find clarity and peace in You. Use me, Lord, to*
> *encourage and support them in their journey."*

Closing:

> *"I ask all these things in the precious name of Jesus Christ,*
> *my Savior. Amen."*

ADDITIONAL RESOURCES

Books: Suggested readings for deeper understanding.

"The Purpose Driven Life" by Rick Warren
This bestselling book offers a 40day spiritual journey that will help you discover and live out God's purpose for your life. It provides practical insights and biblical principles to guide you in understanding your identity and calling.

"Identity: Discover Who You Are and Live a Life of Purpose" by T.D. Jakes
In this empowering book, T.D. Jakes explores the concept of identity from a biblical perspective, encouraging readers to embrace their God-given identity and live out their unique purpose with confidence and conviction.

"Who Am I? Identity in Christ" by Jerry Bridges
This book delves into the biblical truths about who we are in Christ, providing a clear and concise exploration of our identity as believers. It's a great resource for anyone looking to deepen their understanding of their spiritual identity.

"Grace for the Moment" by Max Lucado

This daily devotional offers inspiring and uplifting messages that remind us of our identity in Christ and the grace that sustains us. It's perfect for daily reflections and encouragement.

Articles: Recommended articles for further insight.

"Finding Your Identity in Christ" on Desiring God

This insightful article from Desiring God delves into the importance of finding our identity in Christ rather than in the world. It offers practical advice and biblical wisdom on how to root our sense of self in God's truth.

"Understanding Godly Identity" on Crosswalk

Crosswalk provides a comprehensive article that explores the concept of godly identity, highlighting key scriptures and practical steps to help believers embrace and live out their true identity in Christ.

"Living Out Your Identity in Christ" on Bible Study Tools

This article discusses practical ways to live out your identity in Christ daily, providing actionable advice and scriptural support to help you walk confidently in your faith.

"You Are More Than What You Do: Finding Your Identity in Christ" on Relevant Magazine

Relevant Magazine offers an engaging article that addresses the struggle of defining ourselves by our achievements and encourages readers to find their true identity in Christ.

Online Resources:

Desiring God (www.desiringgod.org)
Desiring God offers a wealth of articles, sermons, and resources focused on helping believers find joy and purpose in God. It's a great site for deepening your understanding of biblical identity.

Crosswalk (www.crosswalk.com)
Crosswalk provides a variety of resources, including articles, devotionals, and videos, to help Christians grow in their faith and understand their identity in Christ.

Bible Study Tools (www.biblestudytools.com)
This site offers extensive resources for Bible study, including articles, commentaries, and study guides that can aid in understanding your identity in Christ.

Relevant Magazine (www.relevantmagazine.com)
Relevant Magazine covers contemporary Christian issues and provides articles that challenge and inspire believers to live out their faith authentically.

These resources will support and enhance your journey of discovering and embracing your identity in Christ. Whether through books, articles, or online resources, you'll find a wealth of knowledge and inspiration to help you grow in your faith and live out your God given purpose.

ABOUT THE AUTHOR

Eric G Reid, Editor in Chief and Co-Founder of Skinny Brown Dog Media

Every day, I wake up with a passion for guiding authors and leaders like you on your journey of discovering and sharing your identity. I'm Eric G Reid, Co-Founder and Editor in Chief at Skinny Brown Dog Media. With over a decade of experience in digital media and publishing, I am dedicated to helping others find their true voice and purpose through the written word.

My journey into the world of publishing began with a simple love for storytelling and a desire to help others tell their stories. As a writer myself, I understand the challenges and triumphs that come with crafting words that resonate. Over the years, I've had the privilege of working with a diverse group of authors, speakers, and coaches, each with a unique voice and message. This experience has taught me the transformative power of words and the importance of sharing our true selves with the world.

As a member of 12Stone Church, my faith plays a central role in my life and work. I believe that understanding our identity in Christ is foundational to living a life of purpose and fulfillment. This belief drives my commitment to helping others discover and embrace their God given identity.

Outside of work, I cherish spending time with my family and my big yellow dog, Max. These moments of rest and connection fuel my passion for helping others. If you would like to connect, feel free to reach out to me at Eric@SkinnyBrownDogMedia.com.

I look forward to joining you on your journey of self-discovery and storytelling.

ABOUT THE WHOLE LIFE DEVOTIONAL SERIES

Welcome to the Whole Life Devotional Series. Think of it as a spiritual road trip through different parts of your faith journey. Each book is like a friendly guide, helping you explore God's love, beef up your faith, and figure out how to live a life that really matters.

I am not about fancy theological jargon here. Instead, I am an authentic voice and practical insights, biblical wisdom, and real-life stories that'll help you grow closer to God. The series is intended to feel like you are a chat with a good friend who just happens to be pretty passionate about personal growth and faith stuff.

Feel free to drop me a line at Eric@SkinnyBrownDogMedia. com. I'd love to hear from you as we dive into this adventure of figuring out who God made us to be. Let's grow together!

Books in the Series

Scheduled Release Early 2025:

Identity: Discovering Who You Are

- Focus: Understanding and embracing your identity in Christ.

- Themes: Self-worth, God's love, being made in God's image.
- Summary: Discover your true identity in Christ and replace the world's misconceptions with the solid truth of God's Word.

Faith: Strengthening Your Relationship with God

- Focus: Deepening your faith and spiritual growth.
- Themes: Prayer, Bible study, spiritual disciplines.
- Summary: Cultivate a vibrant, everyday faith that transforms your life in tangible ways.

Transformation: Embracing Spiritual Growth

- Focus: Becoming more Christlike through spiritual growth.
- Themes: Sanctification, growth in virtues, spiritual maturity.
- Summary: Embrace the process of spiritual transformation and grow deeper in your relationship with God.

Wisdom: Making Godly Decisions

- Focus: Making wise, biblically based decisions.
- Themes: Discernment, moral choices, God's guidance.
- Summary: Learn to make wise decisions that align with God's will and seek His divine guidance.

Surrender: Embracing God's Will

- Focus: Surrendering to God's will.
- Themes: Trust, obedience, letting go, faith.

- Summary: Understand and practice the concept of surrender, letting go of your own plans, and embracing God's perfect will.

Peace: Finding Rest in a Busy World

- Focus: Finding true rest and peace in God.
- Themes: Stress management, trust in God, spiritual rest.
- Summary: Find peace and rest through trust in God and learn practical steps to manage stress and embrace spiritual rest.

Additional books in the series are currently under consideration by the publisher. Please follow for updates and announcements on upcoming releases. Stay connected and be the first to know about new titles and insights designed to deepen your spiritual journey.

I AM

A CHILD OF GOD:
*"See what great love the Father has lavished on us,
that we should be called children of God! And that is what we are!"*
—1 John 3:1

MADE IN GOD'S IMAGE:
*"So, God created mankind in his own image,
in the image of God he created them; male and female he created them."*
—Genesis 1:27

A NEW CREATION:
*"Therefore, if anyone is in Christ, the new creation has come:
The old has gone, the new is here!"*
—2 Corinthians 5:17

CHOSEN AND LOVED:
*"For he chose us in him before the creation of the world to be holy
and blameless in his sight. In love he predestined us for
adoption to sonship through Jesus Christ, in accordance
with his pleasure and will."*
—Ephesians 1:45

GOD'S WORKMANSHIP:

"For we are God's handiwork, created in Christ Jesus to do good works,
which God prepared in advance for us to do."
—Ephesians 2:10

PART OF A ROYAL PRIESTHOOD:

"But you are a chosen people, a royal priesthood, a holy nation,
God's special possession, that you may declare the praises of him
who called you out of darkness into his wonderful light."
—1 Peter 2:9

A FRIEND OF JESUS:

"I no longer call you servants, because a servant does not know
his master's business. Instead, I have called you friends,
for everything that I learned from my Father I have made known to you."
—John 15:15

A TEMPLE OF THE HOLY SPIRIT:

"Do you not know that your bodies are temples of the Holy Spirit,
who is in you, whom you have received from God?
You are not your own; you were bought at a price.
Therefore, honor God with your bodies."
—1 Corinthians 6:1920

MORE THAN A CONQUEROR:

"No, in all these things we are more than conquerors
through him who loved us."
—Romans 8:37

AN HEIR WITH CHRIST:

"Now if we are children, then we are heirs—heirs of God and coheirs with Christ, if indeed we share in his sufferings in order that we may also share in his glory."

—Romans 8:17

THE LIGHT OF THE WORLD:

"You are the light of the world. A town built on a hill cannot be hidden."

—Matthew 5:14

THE SALT OF THE EARTH:

"You are the salt of the earth. But if the salt loses its saltiness, how can it be made salty again? It is no longer good for anything, except to be thrown out and trampled underfoot."

—Matthew 5:13

A LEADER OF MEN:

"And the Lord's servant must not be quarrelsome but must be kind to everyone, able to teach, not resentful."

—2 Timothy 2:24

HIS BELOVED:

"The LORD your God is with you, the Mighty Warrior who saves. He will take great delight in you; in his love he will no longer rebuke you, but will rejoice over you with singing."

—Zephaniah 3:17